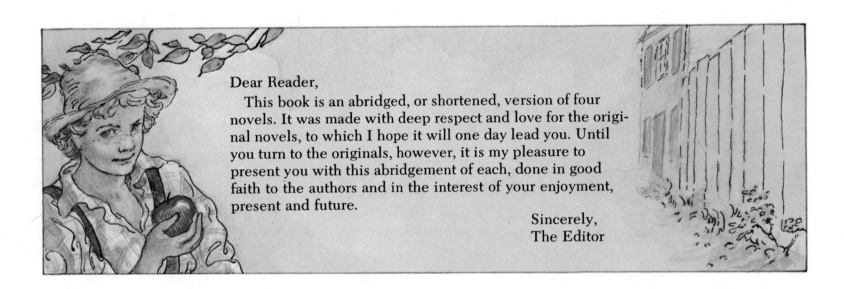

Dear Reader,

This book is an abridged, or shortened, version of four novels. It was made with deep respect and love for the original novels, to which I hope it will one day lead you. Until you turn to the originals, however, it is my pleasure to present you with this abridgement of each, done in good faith to the authors and in the interest of your enjoyment, present and future.

Sincerely,
The Editor

Designed by Robin Battino, A Good Thing, Inc.

CLASSICS

A Child's Introduction to

Treasure Island
Robert Louis Stevenson

6

Black Beauty
Anna Sewell

20

The Adventures of Tom Sawyer
Mark Twain

34

Robin Hood
Henry Gilbert

48

Adapted by Beverly Reingold
Illustrated by Kinuko Craft

Platt & Munk, Publishers/New York

Treasure Island

The adventure which made me, Jim Hawkins, the happiest boy ever to go home again, began at that very place, the Admiral Benbow. It was there, at my father's inn, that I first saw Billy Bones.

I remember him as if it were yesterday, as he came slowly up to the inn door, his sea chest behind him in a handbarrow. I remember him looking round the cove and breaking out in an old sea song:

> "Fifteen men on the dead man's chest—
> Yo-ho-ho, and a bottle of rum!
> Drink and the devil had done for the rest—
> Yo-ho-ho, and a bottle of rum!"

Satisfied that he had found a lonely spot on the coast where he could safely pass the time, Billy Bones rapped on the inn door, and my father let him in. "This is the berth for me," he said.

Billy Bones was a private man. All day he hung round the cove or on the hills with a brass telescope. All evening he sat in a corner of the parlor drinking rum and water. He made it clear that he wanted no company, and people soon learned to let him be.

My friendship, though, Billy Bones did want. He needed my help in avoiding seamen, all of whom he seemed to fear. One in particular, "a seafaring man with one leg," he even paid me to watch for.

For many months, Billy Bones stayed at our inn. Even when he could no longer pay, my father let him have bed and board, for Billy Bones was a terrifying man.

Often he would drink more than his head could carry. Then he would force the company to listen to his frightful sea stories and make the house tremble with "Yo-ho-ho, and a bottle of rum."

The only man who was not afraid of Billy Bones was Dr. Livesey, who came often when my father became seriously ill. One day, when Billy Bones was drunk, he threatened Dr. Livesey with a knife. "If you do not put that knife away this instant," said the doctor, who was also a magistrate, "you shall hang." Grumbling like a beaten dog, Billy Bones put up his weapon.

One morning not long afterward, a stranger approached as I was setting the breakfast table for Billy Bones. "Is this here table for my mate Bill?" he asked with a kind of leer. When I realized the man was looking for Billy Bones, I told him that Billy Bones was out walking. "Well," said the man in a menacing yet anxious manner, "we'll just wait for him."

When Billy Bones returned and saw the stranger, he gasped, "Black Dog!" Then the two old shipmates sat at the table and argued in low voices. Suddenly, they broke into a fight. After a great struggle, Black Dog ran out, crying in agony.

"Are you hurt?" I cried, turning to Billy Bones.

"I must get away from here," he replied. "But first—rum!"

I ran to fetch it, but while I was out I heard a thud in the parlor. Running back in, I saw Billy Bones lying full length on the floor. Just then, Dr. Livesey, on a visit to my father, walked in.

"Oh, doctor, " I cried, "is he wounded?"

The doctor became annoyed. "This man is no more wounded than you or I," he said. "He's had a stroke, as I said he would if he continued drinking."

Later that day, when I visited Billy Bones in his sickbed, he told me about Black Dog. Black Dog had been a member of the old crew of Captain Flint, the pirate. So had Billy Bones. But Billy Bones was the only crew member to whom Flint, as he lay dying, had revealed the location of the treasure he had found on their last voyage out. The rest of the crew were now after Billy Bones, who was waiting fearfully for the black spot, or summons.

That night my father died, leaving only my mother and

me. In my distress, I forgot all about Billy Bones. And it was not until the day after the funeral that he became again an object of my interest.

At about three o'clock that afternoon, as I was standing at the inn door thinking sad thoughts about my father, I saw someone coming slowly near along the road. He was plainly blind, for he tapped before him with a stick and wore a big green shade over his eyes and nose. He was hunched, as if with age or weakness, and he wore an old, ragged seacloak with a hood that made him look positively deformed. I never in my life saw a more dreadful looking creature.

The blind man stopped a little before the inn and called out, "Will any kind friend inform a poor blind man where he may be?" I answered him, upon which the horrible creature asked to be led inside. I held out my hand and found it in a grip like a vise.

"Now, boy," he said, "take me to Billy Bones."

"Sir," I said, "I dare not." But I could not resist the man, for whenever I tried, he wrenched my arm so painfully that I thought I would faint.

Billy Bones lay in his sickbed and was, despite the doctor's orders, drunk as usual. But on seeing the visitor, he became instantly sober.

"Now, Bill," said the blind man, "stay where you are. Boy, take his left hand and bring it to my right."

We both obeyed him, and I saw him pass something to Billy Bones. Then he turned and walked out. I could hear his stick go tap-tap-tapping into the distance.

When Billy Bones and I had recovered our senses, we discovered the black spot in the palm of his hand.

"Ten o'clock!" he cried. "They'll be here in six hours!" He sprang to his feet. As he did, he reeled, swayed for a moment, then fell to the ground—dead.

I immediately realized the danger my mother and I were in, and I lost no time in telling her the whole story. We ran to our neighbors for help. But the very name of Captain Flint frightened them, and not one would stand by us when the pirates returned.

Alone, we rushed back to the Admiral Benbow and Billy Bones. We bolted the door and drew the blinds. Then, gathering my courage, I searched the dead body for the key to Billy Bones's sea chest.

With the key in hand, my mother and I hurried upstairs to the room where Billy Bones had slept. We opened the chest and found, to our surprise, nothing of great value. We took only a bundle of papers tied in oilcloth. And then, on hearing the blind man's stick, we ran for our lives.

We did not get far before, from our hiding place, we could see seven or eight men running up to the inn. Two of them were leading the blind man.

Four or five men broke into the inn and found the dead Billy Bones. They bounded up the stairs to his room.

Soon one of the men shouted to the blind man in the street: "Pew, they've been here before us."

"It's those people of the inn. It's that boy. I wish I had put his eyes out. Scatter, lads, and find 'em."

But before they could do so, a warning shot came from one of their own men. A moment later, there followed the sound of horses galloping. The pirates ran off, leaving Pew helpless. As the riders approached, Pew sought to escape. Instead, he headed straight for an oncoming horse. The rider tried to avoid him, but in vain.

Mother and I came out of our hiding place to speak with the riders, who had been brought to our rescue by a neighbor. After examining the situation, they asked what the pirates could possibly have been looking for, since Billy Bones's money had been left untouched.

"I think I have it in this oilskin," I said. "I am now going to take it to Dr. Livesey."

I found Dr. Livesey at the home of Squire Trelawney. When I had told him of the evening's events and those which had led to them, the doctor took the oilskin packet and opened it. Inside, he found a map showing the location of Captain Flint's buried treasure.

Before anyone could even blink, the squire was making plans to go after the treasure. "Livesey," he said, "you'll give up your practice at once. Tomorrow I start for Bristol. In ten days, we'll have the best ship and crew in England. Hawkins shall come as cabin boy."

With the help of a friend, Squire Trelawney found and bought a ship. The same friend hired a captain. But it was chance, or so it seemed, that provided most of the crew.

One day, as the squire was standing on the dock, a one-legged sailor approached him. The man kept a tavern, but he wanted to return to sea and asked to be taken on as cook. The squire, out of pity, hired him on the spot.

Before long, Squire Trelawney discovered that he had engaged more than a cook. For Long John Silver, as the man was called, soon rounded up a crew of the toughest

old salts imaginable.

Several weeks after we had last seen the squire, Dr. Livesey received a letter from him. It had taken longer than he had expected, but all was ready. Dr. Livesey and I went to Bristol.

The day before we set sail, the squire gave me a note to take to Long John Silver at his tavern. I had no trouble finding the man. His left leg was cut off close to the hip, and under his shoulder he carried a crutch, which he handled wonderfully well, hopping about on it like a bird. He was tall and strong, with a face as big as a ham—pale and plain, but intelligent and smiling.

Now, to tell the truth, from the first mention of Long John in Squire Trelawney's letter, I had become afraid that he might be the one-legged sailor I had watched for at the old Benbow. But one look at the man before me was enough. I trusted him. I plucked up my courage at once and walked right up to Long John Silver.

"Mr. Silver, sir?" I asked, holding out the note.

"Yes, my lad," he said, "such is my name, to be sure. And who may you be?"

Then he saw the squire's letter and started.

"Oh!" he said, quite loudly, and offered his hand.

"You are our new cabin boy. Pleased am I to meet you."

Just then, one of the customers at the far side rose suddenly and dashed out the door. He was quick, but that very quickness attracted my attention, and I looked in time to see that it was Black Dog.

"Oh," I cried, "stop him! It's Black Dog!"

"I don't care who he is," said Silver. "But he hasn't paid. Harry, run and catch him."

I told Long John that Black Dog was one of the pirates. He quickly sent another man after him.

My suspicions were reawakened on finding Black Dog at the tavern, and I watched Long John closely. But he was too clever for me, and by the time the two men had come back out of breath, confessed they had lost Black Dog in the crowd, and been scolded for losing him, I would have sworn to the innocence of Long John Silver.

Later that day, the squire and Dr. Livesey took me to see the ship, the *Hispaniola*. While we were together, Captain Smollett approached the squire.

The captain complained of a lack of discipline among the men. He said they did not respect his orders. And they were holding firearms. In other words, Captain Smollett feared a mutiny and wanted us all on guard.

The next day, after much rejoicing, the *Hispaniola* set sail. I was unimaginably thrilled, for it was my first sea voyage. I enjoyed not only the sea life but also the company, and Long John's especially. "Come away, Hawkins," he would say, "and have a yarn with John. Nobody more welcome than yourself, my son." And then, with his parrot perched noisily on his shoulder, he would spin his yarns.

Soon the first part of our adventure was near an end. We expected to sight land some time that night.

After sundown, when all my work was done, I thought I would like an apple, and I went on deck to the apple barrel. I got bodily into it and found there was scarce an apple left. But instead of getting right out, I settled down and fell asleep.

Suddenly, the barrel shook as a heavy man sat down nearby. I was about to jump out, when I heard the man speak. It was Long John Silver.

"No, not I," said Silver. "Flint was cap'n. I was quartermaster. The same broadside I lost my leg, old Pew lost his headlights. But the *Walrus*, amuck with blood and fit to sink with gold, sailed safe home.

"And that's how we'll go home, men, safe and busting with gold. Here's a first-rate seaman, Cap'n Smollett, sails the blessed ship for us. Here's this squire and doctor with a map and such. I mean this squire and doctor shall find the stuff and help us get it aboard, by the powers. Then—well, dooty is dooty, mates. I give my vote—death."

Before Long John could say another word, I heard the lookout shout: "Land ho!" In the confusion that followed, I slipped out of the barrel and made straight for my friends. As soon as I was near enough not to be overheard, I said, "Doctor, let me speak. Get the captain and the squire down to the cabin, and then send for me. I have terrible news."

When I had told my story, my friends quickly sized up the situation and made plans. We were seven, counting the few faithful hands, to the enemy's nineteen, so we would have to win with our wits.

The next day, because the men were sullen and irritable, the captain allowed them to go ashore. Thirteen went. I decided to join them and hid in one of the boats. Long John saw me and called out to me. But my boat reached shore before the others, and I gave him the slip. With a great sense of adventure, I ran off.

I soon reached a long thicket of trees. On hearing the sound of voices, I crawled under cover.

From my hiding place, I heard the last cry of a man Long John Silver had ordered killed. And I actually saw him kill another. Now I knew the lengths to which this man would go. Two men slain for wanting out. Might I not come next? I took off running.

Without knowing where I was going, I kept running. When I finally stopped for breath, I found myself in an entirely different part of the island. There a fresh alarm brought me to a standstill with a thumping heart.

From the corner of my eye, I saw a figure leap from behind the trunk of a pine. What it was, whether bear or man or monkey, I could not tell. I tried to get away, but it cut me off. As we came face to face, I saw it was a man. Suddenly, he threw himself on his knees and held out his clasped hands.

"Who are you?" I asked.

"Ben Gunn," he answered, and his voice sounded hoarse and strained. "I'm poor Ben Gunn, I am, and I haven't spoken with a man for three years. I was marooned, lad, left here by my shipmates to die. Now, lad, tell me that ain't Flint's ship."

I knew then that I had found an ally. I told Ben Gunn the whole story of the voyage. When I finished, he told me he had been one of Flint's men when Flint had found and buried the treasure.

Ben Gunn and a few other crew members had waited aboard the *Walrus* while Flint went ashore with six men to bury the treasure. Flint came back alone, having killed all six.

Flint would tell no one where he had buried the treasure, but the men, led by Ben Gunn, returned to the island to search for it. They were unable to find anything and held Ben Gunn responsible. They decided to make Ben Gunn pay by leaving him on the island.

During his stay on Treasure Island, Ben Gunn had found the buried treasure. He asked me if I thought the squire would give him his fair share plus passage home if he revealed its location.

"I am sure he would," I said. But before we could exchange another word, we heard the sound of cannon fire, followed by a volley of small arms. We started running toward the anchorage.

Before we had run very far, I stopped short. Just in front of me, I saw a stockade, over which our flag was

waving. At first I thought it might be the pirates, but Ben Gunn assured me they would never hoist the Union Jack.

"Come on, Ben," I cried. But he would not face the squire and the doctor until he was sure they would honor his request. So I went alone to the wall of the stockade and scrambled over it as quickly as I could.

My friends were overjoyed to see me, and you can imagine my happiness at being among them again. The doctor immediately told me what had led to their moving into the stockade on Treasure Island.

Shortly after I left the *Hispaniola*, my friends discovered I had gone. The doctor, knowing the temper the pirates were in, went ashore to see what he could find out. On landing, he checked the stockade marked on the map and determined it would be the best place from which to fight the pirates.

He decided to move in right away. He returned to the ship and picked up the rest of our men, who at the last moment grew in number by one, a pirate named Gray having changed sides. He also picked up arms and supplies.

On their way to the island, the men realized they had

forgotten to destroy the cannon on the ship. And soon they were being shot at by the five pirates who had remained aboard. The squire returned the fire. He aimed for Israel Hands, the gunner, but hit someone else instead. Hands continued firing. He finally struck the boat, and it sank slowly. Fortunately, it was in only three feet of water at the time, so the men were able to wade ashore, carrying whatever they could save.

As they reached the stockade, though, they came upon seven pirates. They opened fire and killed one, scattering the rest. But before they could rejoice in their success, Tom Redruth was shot. They carried him to the stockade, where he died.

I reached the stockade just in time to help bury poor Tom. Then I joined the others in taking stock of the situation. We were now seven (having gained one man and lost one) against fourteen. But we considered our strength greater than it seemed, for we had a strong ally—drink, to which the pirates were easy prey.

Early next morning, I was awakened by a shout. "Flag of truce!" I heard someone say. "Silver himself!"

Sure enough, it was Long John come to make a deal with the captain. Captain Smollett met him just within

the stockade wall. Grumbling because the captain forced him to sit outside on the cold sand, Long John Silver offered his terms for peace.

"Now," said Long John, "here it is. You give us the chart to get the treasure by, and we'll offer you a choice. Either you come aboard once the treasure's shipped, and then I'll clap you somewhere safe ashore. Or, if that ain't to your fancy, you can stay here. We'll divide stores with you, man for man, and I'll speak to the first ship I sight and send 'em here to pick you up."

"Very good," said the captain. "Now you hear me. If you come up one by one, unarmed, I'll clap you all in irons and take you home to a fair trial in England. If you don't, I'll see you all to Davy Jones.

"These're the last good words you'll get from me, for I'll put a bullet in your back when next we meet. Now tramp, my lad, and double quick."

With a dreadful oath, Long John stumbled off. We all returned to the posts we had deserted to listen to the captain and Long John. And we did so immediately, for we expected an attack.

Finally, it came. With a shot by our man Joyce and a shout that they were coming from all sides, we were warned. The pirates were quickly upon us. And we were soon fighting hand to hand within the stockade.

The battle was brief but furious. Joyce and Hunter were killed, and the captain was seriously wounded. But the pirates lost five men, leaving us at four fighting men to nine.

Things were pretty quiet after that. Dr. Livesey tended the wounded and then went off to find Ben Gunn. I got bored and restless and began to envy the doctor being outside. I decided to sneak out for a look around. Then I had an idea. Ben Gunn had told me of a small boat he had made. I would find the boat and paddle it out to the Hispaniola.

With great difficulty, for I did not know the ways of Ben Gunn's boat, I made my way out to the ship under cover of darkness. I cut the line that held the anchor and set the Hispaniola adrift. Then, curiosity getting the better of me, I climbed up that very line to see what was happening on board. Down in the cabin, I saw Israel Hands and a shipmate, both drunk, locked in a deadly wrestle.

I did not stay for the outcome. I returned to my boat and tried to get back to the island. Try as I might, though, I could not control the boat. The current was strong and would have its way. Exhausted, I lay down flat in the bottom of the boat, fell asleep, and dreamed of the Admiral Benbow.

I awoke in the morning to find the *Hispaniola* floating nearby. By the way she was drifting, I could tell no one was steering. I made straight for the ship. With great effort I approached, and with great luck I managed to board her. In the process, however, I lost Ben Gunn's boat and was stranded on the *Hispaniola*.

On board, my eyes met with the greatest disorder I have ever seen on a seagoing vessel. It was obvious that drink and the devil had done their share. Two bodies lay across the deck, and it was some time before I realized one of them was still alive, if badly wounded. It was Israel Hands.

"Mr. Hands," I said, after bringing him some brandy, "I've come aboard to take possession of this ship. You'll regard me as captain until further notice."

Hands looked at me sourly but said nothing. Then he tried to strike a bargain.

"Now look here," he said, "you gives me food and drink and a old scarf or ankecher to tie my wound up, you does, and I'll tell you how to sail her." That seemed fair enough to me.

Later, when we were well on our way to the island, Israel Hands asked me to go below and get him some wine, since the brandy was too strong for him. I did not for a moment believe in his preferring wine to brandy, and I knew that he just wanted me out of sight. But I went along in order to find out what his scheme was. I disappeared to a spot from which I could observe him.

I saw the old gunner rise to his hands and knees and, though his leg hurt sharply when he moved, drag himself across deck at a good rate. In half a minute he had reached a coil of rope and pulled a knife from it. He hid it in his jacket and returned to his old place.

That was all I needed to know. The victim was plainly to be me. Quickly, I fetched the wine. For the time being I was safe, for I knew he wouldn't try anything until the ship was beached.

It was not long before, with Israel Hands's expert

guidance, I managed to get the ship ashore. In the excitement of doing so, however, I dropped my careful guard. I was not prepared when Israel Hands stole up behind me with the knife. If I had not seen his shadow, I would have been a dead man.

My escape was not to be easy. Though wounded, Hands put up a fearful fight. It was only when I remembered my pistols that I felt safe. I pulled them from my pockets.

"One more step, Mr. Hands," I said, "and I'll blow your brains out!"

But before I could fire a shot, something sang like an arrow through the air. I felt a blow and then a sharp pain, and there I was, pinned by the shoulder to the mast. In the surprise of the moment, both my pistols went off and dropped from my hands. But they did not fire in vain. With a choked cry, Israel Hands plunged headfirst into the water.

Fortunately, my wound was shallow, and the knife held me mainly by the shirt. With one jerk, I was able to free myself. I went below deck and bandaged my wound. Then I prepared to leave the ship.

I made my way back to the dark stockade. The men were keeping a bad watch, so I got in easily. I decided to go quietly to sleep and surprise my friends in the morning. But the surprise was mine. Before I could move, Long John Silver had one arm firmly around me.

When a torch had been lit and the men roused, I saw there were seven pirates, two from the boat having earlier joined the five who had survived the battle at the stockade. I asked about my friends. Long John said they had bargained with the pirates when they realized the ship was gone. As a result, the pirates had moved into the stockade and my friends had moved out in safety.

"And lest you should take it into that head of yours," he went on, "that you was included in the treaty, you wasn't. That doctor is mighty fed up with you. So, Jim, will you jine with Captain Silver?"

By that time I was pretty mad. So I told them all how it was me who had overheard them from the apple barrel and warned my friends, how it was me who had cut the cable on the ship and killed a man aboard, and how it was me who was having the last laugh. I said I was as scared of them as of a fly. They could kill me and do

themselves no good—or spare me and keep a witness to save them from the gallows.

Then it was their turn to be angry. One of them whipped out his pistol, and if it hadn't been for Long John, he would have killed me then and there.

I think Long John saw the sense of what I was saying. Things were looking pretty bad for them, and if they did get back, it probably would be to hang. With a good word to Dr. Livesey, Long John knew I could help him.

If protecting me from the pirates would save him later, though, it was getting Long John Silver into hot water now. The men were ready to mutiny. They backed off to talk it over.

Meanwhile, Long John and I had a talk. Surprisingly, Long John admitted he was scared of hanging and needed me as much as I needed him. But the greater surprise was something else Long John told me, something that none of the men knew yet—Dr. Livesey had given Long John Silver the map!

Soon the men approached. They handed Long John a piece of paper with the black spot on it. They were ordering him to step down as captain.

The pirates then spelled out their complaints against Long John. They were angry with him for many reasons but mainly because they had nothing to show for all they had gone through. At that, Long John threw the map at their feet. He was immediately made captain again. And all were making plans to go after the treasure.

In the morning, to my great surprise, Dr. Livesey arrived to tend a wounded pirate. He was still acting as ship's doctor, though he was clearly taking his life in his hands to do so here.

The doctor was equally surprised to see me. I could tell that he was annoyed with me but had not completely lost faith in me. As he was leaving, he asked to speak with me alone. The pirates said no, but Long John whispered that I could talk with the doctor if I gave my word not to run away. I did.

I was only too happy to speak with Dr. Livesey. I told him all about my adventures. When he realized the ship was safely anchored, he asked me to run away with him. But I had promised Long John, and I could not go back on my word. So Dr. Livesey shook my hand, nodded to Long John, and set off into the wood.

After we had had breakfast, Long John Silver, with me strapped to his side, led the last of the pirates in search of the treasure. Everyone but me was in good spirits. Even Long John, I could see, was beginning to have hope of getting the treasure and escaping with his mates to a life of wealth and freedom. I could not understand how my friends could have made this possible by giving him the map.

Before long, we reached the area where the treasure was buried. Then, all of a sudden, the men stopped short and let out a low cry. At the very spot where the treasure was supposed to be buried, there was nothing but a hole. Someone else had found it first.

The tables turned again. The pirates lined up before Long John and me and prepared to shoot. But before they could fire, three shots flashed from the thicket. Three pirates fell, and the rest fled. Dr. Livesey, Gray, and Ben Gunn emerged from the thicket.

Safe at last, Long John and I followed my friends to Ben Gunn's cave. There we found Captain Smollett and the squire. And there we heard the story of how and why my friends had moved out of the stockade and left every-thing to the pirates.

Long before we arrived on the island, Ben Gunn had discovered the treasure. That much I knew. But I did not know that he had carried it back to his cave, bit by bit. When Dr. Livesey found him and heard about this, he decided to move to the cave to keep a closer eye on the treasure. With nothing to lose by giving Long John the map, Dr. Livesey then exchanged it and the stockade for our men's safe passage out.

The next morning, we went to work early. The treasure was vast, and it took days to get it all aboard the *Hispaniola*. Finally, though, we did it. Then, leaving provisions for the pirates who had escaped, we left Treasure Island.

At our first stop on the way home, everyone but Ben Gunn and Long John Silver left the *Hispaniola*. When we returned, Ben Gunn told us Long John had jumped ship. We were delighted to be rid of him so easily.

Some time later, with fresh sailors to man the ship, the *Hispaniola* reached Bristol. Only five men who had sailed out returned with her—"Drink and the devil had done for the rest."

Black Beauty

The first place that I can remember well was a large pleasant meadow with a pond of clear water in it. There, at my mother's side, I spent my earliest years. They were good years, for our master was a kind man.

Before I was two years old, something happened which I shall never forget. I was feeding with the other colts at the lower part of the field, when we heard the cries of dogs in the distance. We immediately cantered off to the upper part, where we could see beyond the hedge to the next field.

There was a hunt in progress. The dogs, followed by a number of men on horseback, were tearing down the field after a hare. The hare tried to get through a fence, but it was too thick. She turned around to make for the road, but it was too late. The dogs were upon her with wild cries.

I was so astonished by this that at first I did not see what was going on by the brook. But when I did look, I found a sad sight. Two fine horses were down. One was struggling in the stream, and the other was groaning on the grass. One rider was getting out of the water. The other lay still on the ground.

"His neck is broken," said my mother, who was now at my side. "I never could understand why men are so fond of this sport. They often hurt themselves, spoil good horses, and tear up the fields, all for a hare or fox that they could more easily get some other way."

The felled rider, son of our neighbor, Squire Gordon, was dead. And the horse that lay groaning on the grass was shortly put out of his misery.

My mother seemed greatly troubled. She said she had known that horse for years. His name was Rob Roy, and he was a good horse. She vowed never again to go to that part of the field.

When I was four years old, Squire Gordon came to look at me. He examined me and said, "When he has been broken in, he will do very well."

My master soon began to break me in. First, he gave me some oats. Then, after a good deal of coaxing, he got the bit into my mouth. It was a nasty thing! But I knew my mother wore one when she went out, and all horses did when they were grown up, and so, with the nice oats, and with my master's kind words and gentle ways, I accepted the bit and bridle.

Next came the saddle, but that was not half as bad. Before long, I was used to wearing it and even to carrying my master upon it.

Also very hard at first was putting on iron shoes. My feet felt stiff and heavy. But this, too, I got used to in time.

Then I was taught to wear a harness and pull a cart or carriage. I did this in double harness with my mother, who could teach me better than a strange horse.

In the spring, a man came to take me to Squire Gordon's at Birtwick Park. There I was placed in a stable, in a large, square stall shut with a gate.

In the stall next to mine stood a fat gray pony with a thick mane and tail, a pretty head, and a pert nose. His name was Merrylegs, and he carried the young ladies of the house.

In the stall beyond was an ill-tempered horse, a tall chestnut mare with a long handsome neck. Ginger, as she was called for her bad habit of biting and snapping, had been abused before coming to Squire Gordon's. But there, like all of us, she was treated well by John Manly, the groom, and James Howard, the stable boy. It was hoped that Ginger would become happier at Birtwick and that her temper would improve.

One morning, after giving me a good grooming, John took me out for a ride. Coming back through the park, we

met the squire and Mrs. Gordon out walking.

"Well, John, how does he go?" asked the squire.

"First-rate, sir," answered John. "He is as fleet as a deer and has a fine spirit, too. But the lightest touch of the rein will guide him. I can see he has not been frightened or ill-used."

The squire and his wife were pleased. "He really is handsome," said Mrs. Gordon. "What do you say to calling him Black Beauty?"

Later, when John returned to the stable, he told James my name. "If it were not for bringing back the past," said James, "I would have named him Rob Roy, for I never saw two horses more alike."

"That's no wonder," said John, "since they both had the same mother."

So poor Rob Roy who was killed at the hunt was my brother! And that was why my mother was so troubled.

One Sunday, Ginger and I were standing alone in the shade of the orchard. Ginger wanted to know all about my bringing up and breaking in, and I told her.

"Well," she said, "if I had had your upbringing, I might have as good a temper as yours, but now I don't believe I ever shall. You see, I never had anyone, horse or man, that was kind to me or that I cared to please.

"Breaking in was the worst time for me. Several men came to catch me. One took hold of my forelock. Another took hold of my nose and held it so tightly I could hardly breathe. Then another took my jaw in his hard hand and wrenched my mouth open. And so by force they got on the bridle and got the bit into my mouth. That was my first experience of men's kindness. It made me bitter.

"My master, Mr. Ryder, could have brought me round. But he had entrusted me to his son's care and only came at times to oversee. His son was a tall, strong, bold man named Samson, who boasted that he had never found a horse that could throw him.

"Early one morning, after having exhausted me the day before, Samson came for me with a saddle and bridle and a new kind of bit. He had just mounted me on the training ground when something I did put him out of temper. He chucked me hard with the rein. The new bit was painful, and I reared up suddenly. This made him still angrier, and he began to flog me. I felt my whole spirit set against him. I began to kick and plunge and rear as I had never done before, and we had a regular fight. Finally, after a terrible struggle, I threw him off backwards. Then I galloped to the other end of the field. I turned and saw him slowly rise and leave.

"For a long time, no one came for me. The sun was hot and the flies swarmed around me, settling on my bleeding flanks where the spurs had dug in.

"At last, just as the sun went down, my master came and gently led me back to the stable. At the door stood Samson. 'Stand back,' said the master, 'and keep out of her way. You've done bad by this filly.'

"Afterward, the master came often to see me. When my mouth was healed, another breaker trained me. He was thoughtful, and I soon learned what he wanted.

"Then I was sold to a fashionable gentleman in London, who made me wear a tight bearing rein. You cannot imagine how it is to have your head held high for hours, your neck aching until you cannot bear it.

"After that I had still more thoughtless masters. Finally, I came here. This is different, of course, but who knows how long it will last."

I was sorry for Ginger, but I knew little then and thought most likely she made the worst of it. However, I noticed as the weeks went on that she grew more gentle and cheerful, and lost the watchful, defiant look she used to turn on any stranger who came near her.

Our master had two other horses that stood in a separate stable. One was Justice, a roan cob used for riding or for the luggage cart. The other was an old brown hunter named Sir Oliver.

Once, when we were all out together, I asked Sir Oliver by what accident he had lost his tail, which was only six or seven inches long. "Accident!" he snorted, with a fierce look. "It was no accident! It was a cruel, shameful, cold-blooded act! When I was young, I was tied up and made fast so I could not stir. Then someone cut off my long beautiful tail, through the flesh and through the bone, and took it away."

"How dreadful!" I exclaimed.

"Ah, yes, it was dreadful. And it caused me not only pain and indignity but also great difficulty, for how could I ever brush the flies off my sides and hind legs anymore? And to think they do it for fashion!"

"I suppose it is also fashion that makes them strap our heads up with those horrid bearing reins I was tortured with in London," said Ginger.

"Why is it," I broke in, "that they put blinkers on us?"

"Well," said Justice, "those flaps that cover the sides

of our faces are supposed to prevent horses from seeing things that might make us shy and start. But if we could see all that was around us, we would be less frightened than we are by seeing only little bits that we can't understand."

Just as we were getting angry with human beings, Merrylegs held up his face and said, "I'll tell you a secret. John does not approve of blinkers, and our master is trying to have bearing reins done away with. So let's cheer up and run to the end of the orchard."

Late in autumn, my master had to take a long business journey. John accompanied him, and I carried them in the dogcart. There had been a great deal of rain, and the wind was wild. When we reached the low wooden bridge, the man at the tollgate said the river was rising fast, and he feared a bad night.

On our way home, the storm was much worse. We went along the edge of the wood, where great branches were swaying like twigs.

"I wish we were out of this wood," said my master.

"Yes, sir," said John. "It would be frightful if one of those branches came down on us."

The words were scarcely out of his mouth when with a groan, a crack, and a splitting sound, an oak came crashing down, torn up by the roots. It fell across the road right before us. I stopped still, trembling.

There was nothing we could do, my master and John agreed, but go back to the wooden bridge we had crossed earlier. So back we went.

When we reached the bridge, it was nearly dark. We were traveling at a good pace, but the moment my feet touched the first part of the bridge, I knew something was wrong. I came to a dead stop. "Go on, Beauty," said my master, giving me a touch with the whip. But I would not go. He gave me a sharp cut, and I jumped, but I would not go forward.

At that moment, the man at the tollgate on the other side of the bridge ran out. He was tossing a torch about like a madman. "The bridge is broken in the middle," he shouted, "and if you come on you'll be in the river."

"Dear Beauty," said John. He took the bridle and gently turned me round to the riverside road that would lead us safely home the long way.

Shortly afterward, James Howard prepared to leave us

for another stable, where he was to be groom. Little Joe Green was hired as stable boy.

Joe was a nice, bright fellow, but he had much to learn. At first, Merrylegs was quite put out at being "mauled about," as he said, "by a boy who knew nothing." But toward the end of the second week, he told me confidentially that he thought the boy would turn out well.

Not long after James had left, I was awakened one night by the stable bell. John rushed into the stable. "Wake up, Beauty," he said. "We must ride."

He took me at a quick trot to the door of the Hall, where the squire stood. "Now, John," he said, "ride for your mistress's life. Give this note to Dr. White. Then give your horse a rest at the inn, and be back as soon as you can."

I galloped as fast as I could. After an eight-mile run, we reached Dr. White's door.

"Mrs. Gordon is very ill," John told the doctor, "and the squire wants you to go at once. Here is a note."

"I will go," the doctor replied, "but my horse has been out all day and is exhausted. May I use yours?"

"He has come at a gallop nearly all the way, sir, but if he must, Black Beauty will go till he drops."

In a minute we had left John far behind. But it seemed ages before we reached the Hall.

When at last we did, the doctor was led into the house, and I was taken to the stable. My legs shook under me, and I could only stand and pant. I had not a dry hair on my body, and the water ran down my legs.

Joe Green rubbed my legs and chest, but he did not put my warm cloth on me. He thought I was so hot I would not like it. He gave me a pail of water to drink and some hay and corn to eat. Then, thinking he had done right, Joe went away.

Soon I began to shake and tremble, and I turned deadly cold. I ached all over, and, oh, how I longed for my thick warm cloth.

After a while, I heard John at the door. I gave a low moan. He was at my side in a moment, covering me with cloths and feeding me warm gruel and hot water.

I was ill for a long time, during which my only consolation was the fact that I had saved my mistress's life. But finally I recovered my health. Because of that,

and because Joe Green learned quickly, John forgave him for the harm he had done me from ignorance. And harmony reigned once more at Birtwick.

Soon, though, sad changes were to take place. Our mistress was ill, and the doctor said that only a move to a warmer climate would help her. The news fell upon the household like the tolling of a death bell.

The squire began to make arrangements for leaving England. He sold all his horses. Ginger and I were to go to an old friend, the Earl of W——. Joe was placed elsewhere. John had several offers, but he said he would wait and look around.

And then the last sad day came. Ginger and I carried our master and mistress to the railway station, where Joe and John bid them a tearful good-bye.

Soon John, too, had to leave. He took us to Mr. York, the earl's coachman, and fondly bid us farewell.

Ginger and I did not get a happy start in our new life. Our master's wife was the cause. My lady liked to have her horses' heads held high in a bearing rein, as was the fashion. Her husband explained that I had never worn a bearing rein and that Ginger had not worn one for years,

but she insisted that we be "fit to be seen." However, my lady agreed to let us get used to it by having the rein tightened bit by bit.

I soon understood what Ginger had complained of, and I told her so. "This is not so bad," she replied. "But if they strain me up tighter, why, let 'em look out! I can't bear it, and I won't."

One day, when my lady came down to the carriage in an irritable mood, she snapped at York, "Pull those horses' heads up at once! Let us have no more of this."

York came to me first and pulled my head back, fixing the rein so tight it was intolerable. Then he went to Ginger. She reared up suddenly, and plunged and kicked in the most desperate manner. Then she kicked over the carriage pole and fell down.

I was unbuckled from the carriage and led to my box. I was sore and angry and felt inclined to kick the first person who came near me. Ginger, badly knocked about and bruised, soon followed me to the stable.

Ginger was never put into the carriage again. When she was well of her bruises, one of our master's sons took her for a hunter. I, however, was obliged to go on in the

carriage with a new partner.

Early in the spring, the earl and part of his family went up to London, taking York and some of the horses. Ginger and I were left behind to be ridden.

I was chosen by Lady Anne, one of the earl's daughters. She would often go riding with her cousin Blantyre, who rode a spirited mare called Lizzie.

One afternoon, Lady Anne decided to try Lizzie. "I advise you not to mount her," said Blantyre. "She is too nervous for a lady."

But Lady Anne insisted. So Blantyre placed her carefully on the saddle and then mounted me. As we were moving off, a footman came out with a note that Lady Anne's invalid sister wanted taken to her doctor.

We rode along merrily until we reached the doctor's house. Blantyre alighted at the gate and was going to open it for Lady Anne, but she said, "I will wait for you here." He looked at her doubtfully. Then, saying he would hurry, he went up to the door.

As we were waiting, some cart horses and several young colts came past us in a disorderly manner. One of the colts blundered up against Lizzie. Lizzie gave a vio-

lent kick and dashed madly off. Blantyre ran back to the gate and sprang into the saddle.

Down the smooth road I galloped. But we could hardly gain ground on Lizzie and Lady Anne. Then they turned onto an area of uneven ground, covered with heather and dark green furze bushes, with a scrubby thorn tree here and there.

There we began to catch up. We saw them approach a wide ditch. Surely, I thought, that will stop them. But with scarcely a pause, Lizzie took the leap, stumbled among the rough clods, and fell.

Motionless among the heather, with her face to the earth, lay my poor mistress. Blantyre kneeled down and gently turned her face upward. It was ghastly white, and her eyes were closed.

Two men who had been cutting turf nearby came running up. Blantyre asked one to mount me and ride for the doctor. This he did, and the doctor was soon on his way. Much later, back at the stable, I learned that Lady Anne was not dead and would recover in time.

While York was in London with the master, a man named Reuben Smith was in charge of the stables. Smith

was a good man, gentle and clever in his management of horses. But he had the habit of drink, and now and then, though he had sworn he would drink no more, he would go on a bout. Then he would be a terror to all.

One day, Reuben Smith took me to town on an errand. We stopped at the White Lion Inn. He ordered the groom there to feed me and have me ready for him at four o'clock. Smith did not call for me until nearly nine, and then it was in a loud, harsh voice that he did.

Before we were out of town, Smith pushed me to a gallop, often giving me a sharp cut with the whip, though I was going at full speed. It was dark, and the roads were stony. One of my shoes was loose. The groom had noticed it and told Smith, who said he would take care of it himself. He did not, and now my foot suffered dreadfully.

The pain became intolerable. I stumbled and fell violently on my knees. Smith was flung off with great force. I got up and limped to the side of the road. Smith tried to rise but could not.

It must have been midnight when I heard the sound of horses' feet. It was two of our men in the dogcart. As they reached us, one jumped down and rushed to Smith.

"He's dead," said the man.

Then they both came and looked at me. They saw my cut knees and hoofs, and they understood what had happened. Reuben Smith was taken home to be buried and I to be doctored. I healed but would never be the same again.

For a month or two after, I was left in a small meadow to recover. One day, dear old Ginger appeared. With a joyful whinny I trotted up to her. But I quickly learned it was not for our pleasure that she had been brought to me. Ginger, too, had come for a rest.

All too soon, Ginger and I were separated again. It had been decided that, due to my unsightly knees, I could no longer serve the earl. I was sold to the master of the livery stables.

Before this, I had always been driven by people who at least knew how to drive. But in my new place I was to suffer all kinds of bad and ignorant driving. I was a job horse and was let out to anyone who wanted to hire me.

After many bad experiences, I was rented by a

man who rode me gently and well. He took such a liking to me that he persuaded my master to sell me to a friend who wanted a safe, pleasant horse for riding.

My new master, Mr. Barry, was a businessman who knew little about riding and wanted a horse only for exercise. He hired a groom named Filcher and left me to his care.

Filcher knew his business, and at first all went well. After a while, though, it seemed that my oats came short. Certainly, I did not get more than a quarter of what I should have been given. In two or three weeks, this began to tell on my strength and spirits.

One afternoon, Mr. Barry rode into the country to see a friend of his. This gentleman had a quick eye for horses. After looking me over, he said, "It seems to me, Barry, that your horse does not look well. How do you feed him?"

My master told him. The other shook his head slowly. "I can't say who eats your corn, my dear fellow, but I am mistaken if your horse gets it."

I, of course, knew where my oats were going. Filcher used to come in early each morning with his little boy, who carried a covered basket. The boy would go into the harness room, fill the basket, and leave.

It was not long before my master also knew this. Because of his friend's suspicions, he had the groom watched. And he quickly caught father and son in the act. The boy was let go, but Filcher was sentenced to prison for two months.

A new groom was immediately hired. But he, too, deceived my master. He was a lazy, vain man who spent all his time grooming himself and doing nothing for me. Unfortunately, this was not discovered until I became ill as a result of improper care.

The groom was fired, and I was treated for my ailment. But even though I regained full health, Mr. Barry decided to sell me. He had had enough of grooms.

I was sold to a horse fair, from where, though my chances of ending up in a bad situation were great, I was happily placed. I was bought by a man named Jerry Barker, a cabdriver who lived with his wife and two children in a poor section of London. A closer, happier family than the Barkers I never knew. And they were as good to me as they were to each other.

The first week of my life as a cab horse was difficult. I was not used to London. The noise, the hurry, the crowds of horses, carts, and carriages that I had to make my way through made me feel anxious and harassed. But when I realized I could perfectly trust my driver, I got used to it.

While Jerry and I were waiting for a fare one day, a shabby old cab drove up beside ours. The horse was a worn-out chestnut with an ill-kept coat and bones that showed plainly. The knees buckled over, and the forelegs were unsteady. It was Ginger!

What a sad tale Ginger had to tell. After a year's rest at the earl's, she was sold. For a while she did well. Then the old strain returned. She was given another rest and sold once more. This happened again and again.

"But, Ginger," I said, "there was a time when you stood up for yourself."

"I did once," she replied, "but it's no use. Men are stronger, and if they are cruel there is nothing we can do but bear it until the end. Oh, I wish the end would come. I have seen dead horses, and I know they do not suffer."

I put my nose up to hers, but I could say nothing to comfort her. Just then, her driver came up. He tugged at the reins and drove her away.

A short time afterward, a cart with a dead horse in it passed our cabstand. The sight was dreadful, and I cannot speak of it. But I believe it was Ginger. I hope it was, for then her troubles are over.

On election day, which we long awaited, Jerry and I were busier than ever. It was quite some time before we could stop for a bite to eat. And before we could finish our meal, our services were required again.

A poor young woman with a sick child stopped to ask Jerry the way to the hospital. Jerry, unwilling to let her walk through the crowds, offered to drive her there.

"No, sir, no. I can't do that," the woman said. "I have only enough money to get back with."

Jerry insisted that she let him take her for nothing. But before the woman and child could step into the cab, two men sprang into it. "This cab is engaged, gentlemen," said Jerry, "by that lady."

"We were in first," said one, "and we shall stay."

The men did indeed stay. But when they realized Jerry would not move the cab, they jumped out in a huff, calling him all sorts of names. Then the woman and child got in, and we took them safely to the hospital.

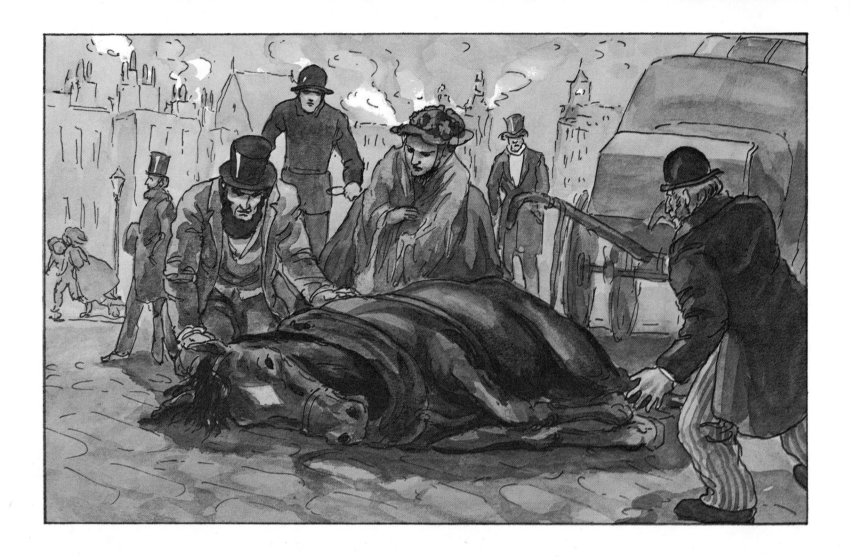

Election day was followed shortly by New Year's Eve. That night, we had to take two gentlemen to a house on one of the West End blocks. We set them down at nine o'clock and were told to come back at eleven. "You may have to wait," they said, "but don't be late."

As the clock struck eleven, we were at the door. The weather was dreadful. A sharp, driving sleet beat down on us, and we were wet and cold. At a quarter past one, the two men came out. They got into the cab without a word of apology and told Jerry where to drive.

At last we got home. Jerry could hardly speak and had a terrible cough. The next day, I learned that he had bronchitis and was in poor condition.

Jerry recovered, but he would never be able to drive a cab again. Luckily, he found employment with his wife's old mistress, who hired him as groom for her stable. The family prepared to move, and another sad parting followed.

My new master was a friend of Jerry's. He was a good man, and I would have found a fine place with him, as Jerry expected, if it had not been for his foreman. This man was always rushing and driving everyone, and in order to save a trip, he would make my carter put more in the cart than I could carry.

Soon I was thoroughly pulled down from carrying overloaded carts. A younger horse was bought to replace me, and I was sold again.

I shall never forget my next master. He had black eyes and a hooked nose, a mouth as full of teeth as a bulldog's, and a voice as harsh as the grinding of cart wheels over gravel. His name was Nicholas Skinner.

Skinner had a low set of cabs and a low set of drivers. He was hard on the men, and the men were hard on the horses.

My life was now so wretched that I wished I might, like Ginger, drop down dead and be out of my misery. One day my wish nearly came to pass.

I was at the train station picking up a party of four—a noisy blustering man with a lady, a little boy, and a young girl. There was a great deal of luggage.

While the man was ordering about the luggage, the young girl came and looked at me. "Papa," she said, "I am sure this poor horse cannot take us and all our luggage so far. He is weak and worn out."

The driver insisted that I could, and the man told the girl to get in and hold her tongue. My young friend had to obey.

I pulled the load as best I could for quite some distance. Then suddenly—I cannot tell how—my feet slipped from under me, and I fell heavily to the ground. Great confusion followed.

I do not know how long I lay there. But when I regained consciousness, I staggered to my feet and was led to a nearby stable.

Nicholas Skinner came to examine me the next day. He decided to give me perfect rest for about ten days and then try to sell me at the fair.

At this sale, I was in company with the old, broken-down horses. I noticed a man coming from the better part of the fair. He looked like a gentleman farmer and had a young boy at his side.

"There's a horse, Willie," said the man, "that has known better days."

"Poor old fellow," said the boy. "Could you not buy him, Grandpa, and make him well again? He seems a very good horse."

The boy persuaded the old gentleman to buy me. And I was taken to a fine home, where my sole duty was to be restored to good health and spirits.

When I was truly my old self again, I was groomed with special care and driven to the home of two elderly women. It seemed they were looking for a safe, gentle horse to pull their carriage. They agreed to have their groom look me over the following day.

The young man arrived early the next morning. At first he looked pleased, but when he saw my knees, he was disappointed. However, he agreed to take me on trial.

Later that day, my new groom came in to clean me. He had hardly begun when he said, "This is just like the star Black Beauty had. White star on forehead, one white foot on the offside, and as I am alive, there is that little patch of white hair John used to call 'Beauty's threepenny bit.' It must be Black Beauty! Why, Beauty, do you know me? I'm Joe Green that almost killed you!" And then he began patting me as if he were quite overjoyed.

That afternoon, the ladies were told about me. They took me out for a ride and decided to keep me.

I have now lived in this happy place a whole year. My work is easy and pleasant. Joe is the kindest and best of grooms. And my ladies have promised that I shall never be sold. I have nothing more to fear. My troubles are over, and I am at home.

The Adventures of Tom Sawyer

Tom Sawyer was a nuisance to his Aunt Polly. He was always getting into mischief. Sometimes Aunt Polly would get angry, but most of the time she would end up laughing. For Tom was also a great joy to her.

One Friday when Tom had played hookey from school, Aunt Polly found out about it at dinner. All the while between dinner and the time that Tom returned from his after-dinner romp, Aunt Polly spent trying to decide whether or not to punish him. But when Tom finally came home torn and dirty, having obviously been in a fight, the matter was settled. He would whitewash the fence on Saturday.

Saturday morning arrived, bright and gay. But Tom's spirits were not in keeping with the day. As he appeared on the sidewalk with a bucket of whitewash and a long-handled brush, his thoughts were all of the fun he had planned for the day. He was a sad figure, indeed.

Tom thought of everything he could do to get out of work. He tried to get Jim, the black boy who worked for Aunt Polly, to whitewash, but Aunt Polly put a stop to that. Then he thought of buying off one of the boys who would soon be coming around to laugh at him. But he had only bits of toys, marbles, and trash in his pocket. At last, though, he had a brilliant idea.

Tom took up his brush and went peacefully to work. Soon Ben Rogers came along.

"Hello, old chap. You got to work, hey? I'm going in a-swimming. Don't you wish you could?"

"What do you call work?" asked Tom coolly.

"Oh, come now, you don't mean to let on that you like doing that?"

But that was exactly what Tom meant to do. And before long, Ben was saying, "Hey, Tom, let me whitewash a little." So Tom did.

After Ben, there were many more who wanted a turn at whitewashing. Tom's work was soon done, and he was free to go and play.

As Tom was passing Jeff Thatcher's house, he saw a new girl in the garden. She was Jeff's cousin, and she had just moved into town with her parents, Judge and Mrs. Thatcher.

Immediately, Tom began to show off. While in the middle of a dangerous gymnastic feat, he noticed that the girl was heading toward the house. Tom's face fell. But his spirits were quickly raised when she stopped on the doorstep and tossed him a pansy.

Monday morning soon arrived. As usual, Tom tried everything to get out of going to school. First he complained of a sore toe. When Aunt Polly took it lightly, he tried a painful tooth. When Aunt Polly took out the loose tooth, he gave up and dragged himself to school.

On his way, Tom ran into Huckleberry Finn, the village outcast. Huck was the son of the town drunkard. He came and went at his own free will. Huck did not have to go to school or church or obey anybody. He never had to wash or put on clean clothes. Nobody forbade him to fight. And he could swear. Huck was the envy of every respectable boy in St. Petersburg.

"Hello, Huckleberry!" cried Tom.

"Hello, yourself, and see how you like it."

"What's that you got?"

"Dead cat. Good to cure warts with. You take it to the graveyard 'long about midnight when somebody that was wicked has been buried. And when it's midnight a devil will come, or maybe two or three. And when they're taking that feller away, you heave your cat after 'em and say, 'Devil follow corpse, cat follow devil, warts follow cat, I'm done with ye!' That'll fetch any wart."

Huck and Tom agreed to meet at midnight to try out the cat. Then Tom ran to school, for he was very late.

On walking into the classroom, Tom was stopped by the schoolmaster, who asked why he was late again. Tom was about to lie when he noticed the new girl sitting next to the only empty seat on the girls' side of the room. He knew that if he confessed, he would be whipped and then made to sit with the girls. So he did.

Before long, Tom and the new girl, Becky, had exchanged names. As soon as Tom learned Becky's name, he wrote her a message on his slate. "I love you," it said. Becky blushed but agreed to meet Tom at lunch.

"Say, Becky," Tom asked when they were alone, "was you ever engaged?"

"No."

"Would you like to be?"

"I reckon so. What is it like?"

"Oh, it's ever so gay! Why, me and Amy—"

"Oh, Tom! Then I ain't the first—"

Becky began to cry. To convince her of his love, Tom took out his favorite possession, a brass knob, and offered it to her. Becky flung it to the floor. Then Tom marched out of the schoolhouse and over the hills, leaving Becky to suffer alone the rest of the schoolday.

Despite his unhappiness, Tom was ready and waiting for Huck at midnight. At the first sound of the signal, he snuck out to meet his pal.

Huck and Tom, being highly superstitious, were more than a little uneasy at the graveyard. Before long, they heard muffled voices. With beating hearts, they watched as vague figures approached.

"It's the devils, sure enough," whispered Huck. "Three of 'em! Lordy, Tom, we're goners! Can you pray?"

"I'll try. Now I lay me down to sleep—"

"Sh!"

"What is it, Huck?"

"They're humans! Why, it's Muff Potter, young Dr. Robinson, and Injun Joe—that murderin' half-breed! I'd druther they was the devils a dern sight. What kin they be up to?"

The three men approached a grave and began to dig. For a long time they worked in silence. At last, they hoisted a coffin from its grave, pried off the lid, and dumped out the body the doctor would use for study. Then they covered it and strapped it to a barrow.

"Now the cussed thing's ready, Doc," said Muff Potter. "But out with another five, or here she stays."

"That's the talk," said Injun Joe.

"Look here, now," said the doctor, "I paid you."

"Yes," said Injun Joe. "And five years ago you drove me from your father's kitchen when I come to ask for something to eat. You said I warn't no good. Now you got to settle."

Injun Joe was threatening the doctor with a fist in his face. The doctor struck out suddenly and knocked him on the ground. At this, Potter leaped to his partner's rescue and struggled with the doctor. Then Injun Joe sprang to his feet, snatching up the knife Potter had brought for digging.

When the doctor knocked down Potter, the half-breed saw his chance. He drove the knife to the hilt in the doctor's breast. The young man reeled and fell partly upon Potter. The two terrified boys went speeding away in the dark.

Injun Joe calmly walked over to the unconscious Potter and put the knife in his open hand. He sat down to wait. Soon Potter began to stir and moan. He sat up and, with a shudder, pushed the body from him.

"Lord, how is this, Joe?" he asked.

"It's a dirty business," said Joe. "Why'd you do it?"

"Oh," groaned Potter, "I'm still drunk. I'm all in a muddle—can't remember anything. Tell me, Joe, did I really do it? I never meant to hurt him."

Injun Joe convinced the innocent man that he had committed a brutal murder. He promised not to betray Potter and sent him scurrying off into the night.

In the meantime, Huck and Tom reached shelter near the village and stopped for breath.

"Do we tell, Tom?" asked Huck.

"What are you talking about? S'pose something happened and Injun Joe didn't hang? Why, he'd kill us. I wish Muff Potter could tell. But he'd just got that whack when Joe done it. Still, we got to keep mum."

The boys swore to secrecy. By then it was almost dawn and time for them to go their separate ways.

Before noon that day, the whole town knew of the murder. School was dismissed, and everyone met at the scene of the crime. Tom and Huck were there. So, to their great surprise, was Injun Joe. But their greatest shock was the sight of Muff Potter, whom everyone was accusing of the crime because he had been seen washing blood from his clothes.

"I never done it, friends," he sobbed, "on my word."

But then Injun Joe betrayed Muff Potter. As he reeled off lie after lie, Huck and Tom stood dumb and staring, waiting for a lightning bolt from heaven to strike the man dead. It never came. Injun Joe walked away a free man, and Muff Potter was carted off to jail.

This was too much for Tom. That morning, he had found the brass knob on his desk at school. Now, beside Becky's rejection, he had an increasingly guilty conscience to cope with. In the depth of despair, he decided to run away.

On his way out of town, Tom ran into his friend Joe Harper. Joe was in the same state of mind, so the two agreed to be pirates together. Then they rounded up Huck Finn and arranged to move to Jackson's Island, a deserted island about three miles below St. Petersburg. This they did late that night on a stolen raft filled with stolen supplies.

In the highest of spirits, Tom Sawyer, the Black Avenger of the Spanish Main, Joe Harper, the Terror of the Seas, and Huck Finn the Red-Handed landed on Jackson's Island at two o'clock in the morning. They built a fire and put some bacon in a pan. After supper, they could only talk about how contented they were.

"A pirate's life is for me," said Tom. "You don't have to get up mornings, and you don't have to go to school and wash and all that blame foolishness."

Joe agreed. And Huck, though he never could complain about civilization, also expressed joy in being as far from it as possible. Then drowsiness overcame all.

The next morning went well, but toward afternoon the boys' spirits began to sink. Homesickness was setting in. Then, from the direction of the very place they were thinking of, came a deep sullen boom.

The boys hurried to the shore nearest town. They parted the bushes on the bank and peered out over the water. In the distance they saw a little steam ferryboat with crowded decks.

"I know!" exclaimed Tom. "Somebody's drownded!"

"That's it!" said Huck. "They done that last summer when Bill Turner drownded. They shoot a cannon over the water, and that makes him come up to the top."

Suddenly, it dawned on all three that they were the victims. They were thought to have drowned, and everyone in town was mourning them. It was worthwhile to be a pirate, after all.

The afternoon wore on and then the evening. Though

still somewhat homesick, Huck and Joe fell into an easy sleep. Tom, however, lay on his elbow for some time, watching the two.

When he was sure they were sleeping, Tom got up carefully and found two large cylinders of thin white sycamore bark. He knelt by the fire and wrote something on each of these. One he put in his jacket pocket and the other in Joe's hat. Then he took off for the water.

Having lost the raft to the current, Tom swam part way. But for the long haul home, he had to sneak aboard a ferryboat on its last trip of the night. Soon Tom was well hidden in Aunt Polly's house, not far from where she sat up late, talking with Joe Harper's mother.

"He warn't bad,"Aunt Polly was saying, "only mis-cheevous. But he never meant any harm, and he was the best-hearted boy ever." She began to cry.

"It was just so with my Joe—always full of his devilment but just as unselfish and kind as he could be." And Mrs. Harper sobbed as if her heart would break.

Before Aunt Polly and Mrs. Harper parted for the night, Tom learned something else beside the fact that he was a wonderful and well-loved young man. It was that on Sunday morning, if the bodies had not yet been found, a funeral service would be held for the boys.

Then Mrs. Harper left, and Aunt Polly went up to bed. When he was sure she was asleep, Tom stole over to her bed and took out the sycamore scroll. But he had a second thought and put it away. He leaned over and gently kissed his aunt. Then he set off in a "borrowed" skiff on the journey back to Jackson's Island.

Tom arrived at daybreak. The boys greeted him warmly and went off to explore while Tom slept. In the afternoon the three ran about gaily, but by evening they were all in the dumps.

Joe was in the worst shape. But when he decided to leave, Huck said he, too, would go. Only Tom held out. However, as the others started off, he ran after them, yelling, "Wait! I want to tell you something!"

The boys stopped. When Tom told them his plan, they let out a whoop of delight. Then all resumed their adventure. In this gay manner, several days passed.

Meanwhile, spirits ran low in the village. The dead boys were on everyone's mind. Becky Thatcher wore one of the saddest faces, and she wished with all her heart that she still had Tom's brass knob.

On Sunday morning, the villagers gathered at church

to pay their last respects to the young men. When the service was well under way, and the congregation was sobbing pretty much in harmony, the church door creaked loudly. The minister raised his streaming eyes to the door. To his shock and that of the entire congregation, whose eyes had followed his, in walked the boys.

Family and friends immediately threw themselves upon the young men with hugs and kisses. Even Huck was lovingly received. Tom's plan for them to come back and attend their own funeral was a great success.

Tom returned to school in a blaze of glory. Becky was once again interested in him and did everything possible to win Tom's attention. But Tom, wanting to make Becky suffer, devoted himself to his old girlfriend. Becky therefore turned to another boy. Thus each succeeded in making the other hurt and angry.

Tom went home for lunch in a dreary mood. And there was his aunt, saying, "Tom, I've a notion to skin you alive!"

"Auntie, what have I done now?" he asked wearily.

It turned out that Joe Harper had told his mother about Tom's visit to Aunt Polly from Jackson's Island. Mrs. Harper in turn had told Aunt Polly. And Aunt Polly felt Tom had made a fool of her.

"Oh, no, auntie," said Tom. "I didn't come over here to laugh at you that night. It was to tell you not to be uneasy about us, because we hadn't drownded."

"Why didn't you, then?" asked Aunt Polly.

"Why, you see, when you got to talking about the funeral, I just got full of the idea of our coming and hiding in the church, and I couldn't bear to spoil it. So I put the bark back in my pocket and kept mum."

"What bark?"

"The bark I wrote on to tell you we'd gone pirating."

Aunt Polly hugged Tom and told him to be off to school. Then she went to the jacket Tom had been wearing when pirating and looked in the pocket. Soon she was reading Tom's bark through flowing tears.

When Tom went back to school that afternoon, he found Becky upset. She had looked at the forbidden anatomy book that belonged to the schoolmaster, Mr. Dobbins, and she had torn a page. Mr. Dobbins would be sure to see it.

Mr. Dobbins came upon the page that very afternoon. He became pale with fury and turned to the class. "Who tore this book?" he asked.

One after another, the students shook their heads as Mr. Dobbins addressed them. Then he got to Becky. Becky wrung her hands and looked away. But just as she was about to confess, Tom shouted, "I done it!"

As always, Tom took his whipping in a quiet and dignified manner. But this time he also took it with pride, because he suffered for Becky. And when Becky said, "Tom, how could you be so noble?" he could not have been happier.

Classes soon ended for the summer, and Muff Potter's trial rapidly approached. Without Becky, who had left on vacation, Tom found time hanging heavy on his hands. The weight of guilt doubled his burden.

To lighten the load, Tom and Huck often went to the jailhouse to visit Muff Potter. But Muff's gratitude only made the boys feel worse.

At last, the trial began. There were many witnesses with evidence against Muff Potter, and not one with a word on his behalf. It was certain that Muff Potter would be convicted. Then Muff's lawyer said, "Call Thomas Sawyer to the stand."

When Tom, looking badly scared, had been sworn in, the lawyer asked, "Thomas Sawyer, where were you on the seventeenth of June, at the hour of midnight?"

Tom glanced at Injun Joe in the audience and his tongue failed him. After a few moments, however, he got his strength back and answered, "In the graveyard."

Then, without mentioning Huck, Tom told the whole story. Suddenly, there was a loud crash! Quick as lightning, the half-breed sprang for a window, and, tearing his way through the crowd, escaped.

Once again, Tom Sawyer was the village hero. But this time a powerful fear dampened Tom's spirits. By day, when Muff Potter showered him with gratitude, he was glad he had done what he did. By night, when Injun Joe haunted his dreams, he was sorry he had ever been born.

Huck also went about in a state of fear. Though Injun Joe's escape had saved him from having to testify in court, the lawyer knew about his role. For Tom had told the lawyer everything the night before the trial.

As the days wore on, Tom's fear lessened somewhat, and his spirit of adventure returned. He decided to go treasure hunting with Huck.

Carrying a pick and shovel, Huck and Tom made their way to the haunted house. After a short peek at

the weed-grown floorless room, with its rickety old staircase and cobwebs everywhere, they tiptoed in.

After a while, the boys went upstairs. They took a quick look around and started to go back down. Then they heard a noise.

"Let's run," said Huck, white with terror.

"Keep still!" Tom replied. "They're coming in."

The boys stretched out on the floor with their eyes to holes in the floorboards and saw two men enter the house. One was a ragged creature they did not recognize. The other was a Spaniard they had seen in town.

The men made themselves comfortable and began talking. As soon as the Spaniard opened his mouth, the boys gasped. It was Injun Joe!

"I'm going to drop into town just once more," said Joe. "We'll do the job after I've spied around and think things look good for it. Then for Texas!"

"Right," said his partner. "Now, what'll we do with the six hundred and fifty in silver we have left?"

"Leave it here. We'll bury it deep."

The men then began to dig a hole for their money. Before long, though, Joe's knife struck something.

"What is it?" asked his comrade.

"Man, it's money."

Injun Joe pulled out a handful of gold coins. He grabbed a nearby pick and looked it over. Then he worked away until he had unearthed the box.

"Pard," he said, "there's thousands of dollars."

"Now you won't need to do that job."

"You don't know me," the half-breed said, frowning. "It ain't robbery—it's revenge. I'll need help."

"Okay," his partner nodded. "But what'll we do with this—bury it again?"

"No," Injun Joe replied. "That pick had fresh earth on it. Someone's been here. Maybe still is. I'll go upstairs and have a look."

The boys could hardly breathe. Steps came creaking up the stairway. Suddenly, there was a crash of rotten timbers, and Injun Joe landed on the ground in the debris of the ruined stairway.

"Ah, well," he said. "If anybody's up there, they can stay. But I don't think there is. Whoever brung those things in here probably caught sight of us and took off running. Now let's get to Number Two with this stuff."

With that, Injun Joe and his partner picked up the box and headed off. The boys, weak but very relieved, left, too. But they did not follow the men. They were happy just to be alive.

The next morning, Tom grabbed a quick breakfast and rushed out to see Huck. He was hoping Huck would say nothing of the night before and thus prove it had all been a bad dream. But Huck's first words were, "Tom, if only they hadn't 'a' seen the tools, we'd 'a' got the money. Oh, ain't it awful!"

When he'd accepted the reality of the situation, Tom decided they would have to find the treasure. Between them, the boys figured out that Number Two was a room in one of the two taverns in town.

Once they had found the hideout, the boys thought of a plan for getting the treasure. Every night Huck would watch the tavern from the alley behind it. If he saw Joe go out, he would signal Tom. Tom would then go in and hunt for the treasure while Huck kept a lookout.

The signal still had not come days later, when Becky Thatcher returned to town and announced that she would be giving a picnic the following day. Naturally, Tom would attend.

The old steam ferryboat was hired for the picnic. Parents were left behind, and a few young ladies and gentlemen went along to look after the younger people. Because the boat would be late in returning, Mrs. Thatcher suggested that Becky stay overnight with one of the girls who lived near the ferry landing. Becky promised to stay with Susy Harper. But later, as the boat moved along, Tom had a better idea.

"Say, 'stead of going to the Harpers', we'll climb right up the hill and stop at the Widow Douglas's. She'll have ice cream, and she'll be glad to have us."

Tom was able to convince Becky that what her mother didn't know wouldn't hurt her, and she agreed to spend the night at the Widow Douglas's.

Several miles below town, the ferryboat stopped at the mouth of a woody hollow and tied up. The children played outside for a while. Then they lit candles and went into McDougal's cave, a huge cavern with tunnels that branched off from all sides.

Because the cave was an unending maze, the children were told to stay in the main cavern. There they played until it was almost dark and time to go home.

As the night wore on, Huck kept his usual watch at the tavern. At eleven o'clock, when he was about to leave, he heard a noise. The alley door closed quietly. Then

two men brushed by him in the dark, carrying what seemed to be a box. No time to call Tom, Huck thought, as he glided softly behind the men.

Before he knew it, Huck was within steps of the Widow Douglas's grounds. So this is where they're going to bury it, he thought. Then Injun Joe spoke. "There's lights," he said. "Maybe she's got company."

Huck immediately realized this was to be the revenge job. He wanted to run. But he remembered that the widow had been kind to him more than once.

"Well," Joe's partner said, "better give it up."

"Give it up," replied Joe, "and maybe never have another chance. Naw! Her husband was the justice that jailed me for a vagrant. He's dead now, so she'll pay."

Huck took one step backward and then another. When he had moved far enough away in this manner, he took to his heels and sped to the Welshman's.

"Let me in!" he shouted. "Quick!"

Because he still feared having anyone know of his involvement with Injun Joe, Huck made the Welshman promise not to reveal his name. Only when the Welshman had done so did Huck tell him what was going on at the Widow Douglas's. The Welshman quickly gathered

his sons and headed for the widow's. Huck returned to town.

Before daylight, Huck went back to the Welshman's.

"I've come becuz I wanted to know about it. What happened?"

"Meanest kind of luck," said the Welshman. "Just as we got up to them, I sneezed. They heard and ran off. We followed, but we couldn't get 'em. Soon's it's light, though, the sheriff's men are going to search the woods."

Huck made the man promise once more not to reveal his name. Then he left.

The day being Sunday, everyone gathered at church. After the sermon, the talk was all of the danger the Widow Douglas had been in the night before. It was, that is, until Mrs. Thatcher asked Mrs. Harper, "Is my Becky going to sleep all day?"

"Becky?" replied Mrs. Harper.

But Becky had not stayed with the Harpers. Nor had Tom, whom Aunt Polly asked about. They both then asked Joe Harper when he had last seen Tom and Becky. Joe could not remember. And neither could the other children. It was dark when they returned from the picnic, and no one had noticed if anyone was missing.

Instantly, two hundred men were rushing down the highroad and river toward the cave. They stayed there for three long days, finding nothing.

In the meantime, Tom and Becky were indeed lost in the cave. At the picnic, they had strayed from the others. When they realized it was time to return, they also realized they had twisted and turned in the tunnels until they no longer knew how to go back.

For what seemed an eternity, Tom and Becky wandered about the cave in search of a way out. They used their candles carefully, but the last bit was soon gone. And, except for a small piece of cake which they quickly ate, they had no food. Becky cried a great deal, and Tom tried to cheer her. But he had no hope himself.

Then Tom had an idea. He took a kite string from his pocket, tied one end to a rock, and, unwinding it as he moved along, went exploring in some nearby tunnels. Becky followed him closely.

Suddenly, not twenty yards away, a hand holding a candle appeared from behind a rock. Tom shouted for joy. Then he realized his mistake—it was Injun Joe! Tom was paralyzed, but Joe ran away. Tom recovered his senses and persuaded Becky that he had seen nothing.

Tom and Becky's hunger soon proved to be greater than Tom's fear of Injun Joe. So once again, but this time alone, Tom took off with the kite string. Finally, his explorations paid off.

In the distance, Tom glimpsed a speck of light and, on moving up to it, found a small hole through which he could see the Mississippi River rolling by. Tom returned for Becky. Then they made their way out of the hole, hailed a passing boat, and went home.

For several days, Tom and Becky were bedridden. When he was able to get up, Tom visited Huck, who was himself in bed at the Widow Douglas's, recovering from a fever which had kept him from learning about Tom and Becky's dilemma. Tom told Huck the whole story.

On his way home from Huck's, Tom stopped off at the Thatchers'. Judge Thatcher told him then that no one else would get lost in the cave, for he had had the cave door bolted. Tom turned white and shouted, "Oh, judge, Injun Joe's in the cave!"

Within moments, a dozen skiff-loads of men were on their way to the cave. When they opened the door, they found Injun Joe. He was dead.

So it was all over. Joe's partner had been found

drowned in the river, and Joe had starved to death in the cave. Of course, the treasure was still missing.

Huck had looked for the treasure at Number Two and found nothing. Tom said he was not surprised, for he was pretty sure Injun Joe had buried it in the cave.

Huck agreed to return to the cave with Tom. They made their way to the place where Tom had seen Joe with the candle. Nearby they saw a huge rock with a cross on it. The boys began to dig. They had hardly worked when they struck wood. They lifted the planks and there, sure enough, was the treasure box.

The boys soon emerged from the cave with their riches. They set it in a wagon and began to move slowly with the heavy weight. As they were passing the Welshman's house, the man came out and said, "Come along with me, boys. Everyone's waiting."

The Welshman helped the boys carry the "old metal," as they called their treasure, and led them to the Widow Douglas's. The widow's house was grandly lit, and many people were there.

After changing into clothes that had been brought for them, Tom and Huck took their places in the dining room. Then the reason for the celebration was made clear. The Widow Douglas was honoring the Welshman for having saved her from Injun Joe.

The Welshman accepted the widow's thanks. But then he turned and pointed to Huck, saying there was the true hero. The widow was overcome with gratitude. She said she would take Huck into her home and educate him. When the time came, she would give him a modest sum of money to start a business.

But it was Tom's turn to spring one. "Huck don't need it," he said. "Huck's rich."

And the boys brought forth the treasure and counted twelve thousand dollars. Once again, they had created excitement that would not soon die down.

Huck moved in with the Widow Douglas. There he was kept clean and neat and forced to eat with a knife and fork. There he had to learn his lessons and go to church. He hated it.

After three weeks, Huck ran away. But Tom soon found him and persuaded him to return to the widow and civilization. For only if he did so would Tom allow him to be part of a new gang. Huck could not resist this, so back he went—provided that Tom have the widow let up on him a bit.

Robin Hood

One summer afternoon, a young man of about twenty-five stood behind a tree in the lush and lonely Barnisdale Forest and looked out into a glade. Suddenly, he heard a quiet rustle from the bushes before him and saw an arrow speed from them straight to a nearby deer.

Before long, the hunter came out from his hiding place and looked around to be sure none of the king's foresters had seen him. Then he walked to where the doe lay and with his knife began to cut feverishly from the tenderest parts of the carcass.

The young man came forth and startled the hunter, who for a moment seemed about to spring upon him.

"Man," he said, "what madness drives you to this?"

The serf recognized the speaker at once.

"Madness!" he said, stuffing meat into his tunic. "'Tis not for myself, Master Robin. My little lad is dying of hunger, and while there's deer in the greenwood he shall not starve."

"Your little lad, Will Scarlet?" asked Robin Hood.

"Aye," replied Will. And then he told Robin his sister's son had come to live with him. Her husband had taken ill and died, and she had been thrown out by the lord's steward to fend for herself. She soon died of hunger, leaving three orphaned children. Gilbert, the youngest, Will Scarlet had taken into his home.

After he had heard this tragic tale, Robin was enraged against the steward, Sir Guy of Gisborne, who ruled the manor of Birkencar for the monks of St. Mary's Abbey. But he knew the steward did no more than the abbot and monks permitted him, and he cursed the whole brood of them, rich and proud and given over to high living on services and rents wrung from the poor serfs.

The year was 1185, and the serfs, who worked the land, were oppressed by the lords and prelates. They suffered most, however, from the harsh laws of Henry II, king of England. One such law prohibited the slaying of the king's deer.

From a little distance before Robin and Will, there suddenly came a noise. Robin stopped and laid his longbow and arrows at the root of an oak. Then he said to Will, "Place the deer's meat beside these. Quick, man, before the foresters see your bulging breast."

Will did as he was told. Then the men resumed their walk. When they had gone a few steps, Will looked back at the place where they had put their things. They were gone!

The next moment, the narrow path before them was blocked by two burly foresters. But for Robin's bold looks as he advanced, the foresters would surely have stopped the men.

As Will and Robin approached the farms of the manor, Will prayed that none had missed him. If his absence were known, the purpose for it would also be known. "At least," he thought, "I have got what I went for—food for my Gilbert."

Then Will remembered that he did not have the meat. At that moment, Robin said carelessly, "Hello, there are my longbow and arrows and your venison, lad."

At the look of fear on Will's face, Robin assured him that it was not evil spirits who had done this thing. "Scarlet," he said, "I think I see a time before us when you and I will be much together in the greenwood. Then I will show you my friends there."

Robin bid Will farewell and turned once more to the greenwood. With a quick and eager step he passed through the glade, for he was going to see Marian, the

lady he loved best in all the world. Marian was an earl's daughter and Robin but a freeman, so her father would not allow them to marry. However, they swore that neither would marry anyone else.

This day Marian was to journey from her father's castle at Malaset to that of her uncle, Sir Richard at Lee, near Nottingham. Robin had promised to guide her through the forest.

As he approached Malaset, Robin came upon a hidden band of men with a knight in their midst. Though he did not recognize them by sight, when the knight spoke Robin knew him and his purpose.

"So, Roger de Longchamp," said Robin to himself, "you would seize by force my lady whose favor you cannot get by fair means!"

Soon the sound of a lady in conversation with her steward was heard over the laughter of the attendants who followed her. The knight and his men quickly burst through the trees. There followed a furious struggle between Marian's men and those of the knight, but the poor attendants with their staffs had little chance against the robbers with swords.

Sir Roger's hand was already on the reins in Marian's fingers when there came a sound like a great bee. Marian looked at the bars of the knight's visor and saw the shaft of an arrow quivering before them.

The knight groaned, swayed, and fell from his horse. His men stopped fighting for a moment, then scattered as more arrows followed.

Then Marian saw Robin come forth from the woods. With flushing cheeks, she said, "Robin! I knew you would not fail me. That was a brave shot which struck down the felon knight. But if he is who I think he is, his death will work you much harm."

Robin smiled. Then quickly and quietly he guided Marian and her party into the depths of the woods and on to Sir Richard at Lee's.

Sir Richard greeted the group warmly. When he heard what had happened, he turned to Robin and said, "You have rid the earth of a vile oppressor, and I thank you heartily. Yet I think of what you may suffer. The comrades of Roger, Isenbart de Belame and the others, will not rest in their efforts to capture you and take you to Wrangby Castle, which men rightly call the Evil Hold."

"Fear not for me," said Robin with a quiet yet firm voice. "But do you and the father of my lady take care those evil knights do not harm Marian. As for me, I will do all I can to shield her."

For three days, Robin stayed with Marian at her uncle's. On the fourth day he returned to the forest. There he met Ket the Troll, one of the friends of whom he had spoken to Will Scarlet. Ket and his brother, Hob o' the Hill, were little people of the forest who became Robin's friends when Robin saved their lives one day. But it was from love and respect more than gratitude that they remained his devoted friends.

"You followed the men that fled," said Robin. "Where went they?"

"To the Evil Hold," replied Ket. "But, Robin," he continued, "you have more to fear than you know. I have spoken with your man Scadlock. He has lately seen Guy of Gisborne riding about your land."

Robin's land lay beside the forest of Barnisdale. It consisted of a house and some hundred and sixty acres of the richest land at the edge of the manor of Birkencar. It was but a small piece of the manor, but the monks of St. Mary's Abbey longed for it.

Robin determined to return home immediately. After bidding farewell to Marian, he headed through the forest. When Robin reached his house, he looked beyond to the cottages of the five serfs who were part of his land. It was very still. There were no children playing before the cottages, and no life stirred within.

Robin walked along until he caught sight of a soldier, one of the men-at-arms of the abbot of St. Mary's. The man's attention was held by something before him.

With the stealthiness of a cat, Robin came up behind the soldier and wound his fingers around the man's throat. When he fainted, Robin bound him.

Then Robin turned to see what had gripped the man's attention. A soft groan escaped his lips. Tied to posts in front of the house were Scadlock and three other serfs. Their backs were bare, and before each stood a burly soldier with a long strap in his hand. A little way from them stood Hubert of Lynn, their chief, a man Robin had long hated for his cruelty. At a word from this man, four whips rose in the air and came down upon the bare backs which, since Robin had been their lord, had never been wealed by the whip.

Robin laid out his arrows and twanged his bowstring. He notched the first shaft and aimed at the breast of Hubert. With a cry, Hubert sank to the ground.

The place hummed with a sound like that of bees, and all the soldiers fell, one after another. Robin hurried down to release his men.

"'Twas but yesterday, master," said Scadlock, when Robin asked what had happened, "that they proclaimed you outlaw for the murder of Roger de Longchamp. This morning Hubert of Lynn came to possess your lands for the lord abbot. We tried to beat him back, but we could not."

Later, when Robin had the serfs together at his dinner table, Scadlock asked, "Master, must it be the woods and the homeless life of an outlaw for you?"

"There is no other way," replied Robin.

"I will go with you, master, and so will the others, for after this day we can expect no mercy from Guy of Gisborne."

Suddenly, they heard the sound of many voices and the tramp of feet coming toward them from across the field. It was a group of serfs from the manor.

"Give them a hearing, Master Robin," said Will the Bowman, one of the older serfs.

"Well, lads," said Robin, "what do you want of me?"

"We would run to the greenwood, master," they cried. "No more can we bear our hard lot."

At that moment, Robin noticed Will Scarlet was not there. "Where are Scarlet and his lad?" he asked.

"Will Scarlet lies in the pit!" said Much, the Miller's son. "He is nigh dead with a hundred lashes. Tomorrow he will lose his right hand for shooting the king's deer."

"That shall not be," cried Robin. "For I will take him from the pit this very night."

"Master," cried the others, "we will go with you."

"Lads," said Robin, "I will be one with you."

"Hold up each your right hand," shouted Will the Bowman, "and swear to be true and faithful till your dying day to our brave leader, Robin Hood."

All held up their hands and solemnly took the oath. Then they followed Robin out of his house and over to the manor house of Guy of Gisborne. The house was dark and silent. Robin signaled the men to wait as he approached the underground prison.

Robin hurried down the flight of steps that led to the prison door. There he saw a small figure crouching at the

52

door. It was Gilbert, crying softly to his uncle. From behind the door could be heard the weak voice of Will Scarlet, saying, "Laddie, go and hide. If Guy catches you here he will beat you."

"Hello, laddie," said Robin.

The boy recognized Robin at once and shouted with delight, "Here is Robin, uncle. I knew he would come."

With two deft blows with his axe and a wrench with his dagger, Robin broke the lock and pulled open the door. Gilbert rushed in and with a knife began to carefully cut his uncle's bonds.

Then Scadlock and two serfs appeared, and at a word from Robin picked up Will gently and carried him out onto the grass. In silent thanks, Will firmly clasped Robin's hands.

Robin turned to Scadlock. "Where are the others?" he asked.

"I know not," replied Scadlock.

Robin hurried off to find the other men. When he did, it was too late to stop them.

"'Tis a serf deed for serfs to do," said Will the Bowman, as he helped light the fire that would burn the manor house and Guy of Gisborne with it. "'Tis our right. In the morning when we're in the greenwood, we'll do your bidding and look to no one else."

"But you must call out the women," urged Robin. This they did, and then all stood and watched the flames.

Suddenly, from the rear of the house came cries of terror. Robin and Will ran around to find the serfs on that side pointing to a distance. They looked and saw what seemed to be a brown horse running away on two feet. With a cry of rage, Will followed it. "Come back!" cried the serfs. "'Tis the Spectre Beast!"

Robin shook his head and walked away, for he knew it was Guy of Gisborne, escaping in a disguise that would frighten the superstitious serfs. Will the Bowman gave good chase but could not overtake the fugitive. And so, partly in victory, partly in defeat, Robin Hood and his band of twenty men hastened in the dark of night to the depths of the forest, where they would make their new home.

Before many days, the men were more at home in the forest than they had ever been elsewhere. And they were happy there, though they still had to work hard.

For Robin knew their lives depended on their learning to use the staff, the sword, and the longbow. And every day he made them practice their skills.

One day, Much, the Miller's son, said to Robin, "Surely now that we are outlaws, you should give us some rule whereby we may know whom we shall beat and bind, and whom we shall let go free."

Robin replied, "I will have you hurt no woman. You may do no harm to any honest peasant who tilleth his soil in peace, nor to any good yeoman. Knights, also, and squires who are proud but are good fellows, you shall treat with kindness. But abbots and bishops, priors, canons, and monks, you may do your will upon. When you rob them of their gold, you are taking only that which they have squeezed from the poor. They preach the teaching of the Lord, but they practice not that which they preach."

"Yea!" shouted the outlaws. "We will take toll from all such who pass through the greenwood."

"Now, lads," Robin went on, "though we be outside men's laws, we are still within God's mercy. Therefore, I would have you go with me to church."

Soon, in single file, the men were following Robin through the forest to a nearby village. At the little wooden church, where they were alone except for the parish priest and a handsome young squire, Robin and his men sat for the service.

The service was but half done when into the church came a little man, slight of form and dark of face. It was Hob o' the Hill. He walked quickly up to Robin and whispered, "Two knights have followed you, master. There are twenty men-at-arms with them. They are within a bowshot of the door."

"Go and watch at the door," said Robin quietly. "I will attend to them when the service is done."

The service went on, but before it could be finished, an arrow sped through one of the narrow window slits and struck the wall.

The outlaws flew to the window slits and prepared for Robin's command to shoot. The young squire approached Robin and asked who might be pursuing him. When Robin replied that it was men of the Evil Hold, the young man said, "Then, good sir, pray let me aid you in this. Isenbart de Belame is my most bitter enemy."

"You may help me," said Robin, "seeing your anger is so great. But who may you be?"

"I am Alan de Tranmire. But by my friends I am called Alan-a-Dale."

"Well, then, Alan-a-Dale, get a spare bow and a bunch of arrows, and join us."

None too soon did Alan take his place among the outlaws, for the men-at-arms were almost upon them. It was only a matter of seconds before Robin shouted, "Shoot!"

Twenty-one arrows flew from the slits and hummed across the space of some sixty feet. Almost simultaneously, ten men fell. The rest fled.

"Follow them, lads," shouted Robin.

Robin turned to thank Alan-a-Dale. "If at any time you should need a few good bowmen," he said, "send word to Robin Hood."

"I thank you, Robin Hood," said Alan. "I may soon have need of your help."

"What!" said Robin with a laugh. "Hath so young and gallant a squire already an enemy?"

"Aye, good Robin," Alan replied. "It is thus. I love a fair maiden, Alice de Beauforest. Her father holds his manor from Isenbart de Belame, who wishes him to marry Alice to a rich old knight who is as evil as Isenbart

himself. Walter de Beauforest would rather wed the lady Alice to myself, but the lord of Belame threatens to bring fire and ruin upon him and his lands."

"Is any time fixed for this marriage?" asked Robin.

"It must be done within a year," Alan replied.

"There is time enow," said Robin. "We shall meet anon and speak of this matter again." Then he left.

Robin headed toward the Stane Lea, where his men were now making their camp. He knew they would be waiting for him after their chase of the men-at-arms.

Robin was almost at the end of his journey when he came to a broad stream that could be crossed only by a narrow beam. It was wide enough for just one man.

Robin had walked two or three feet along the beam when on the other bank a man appeared, jumped on the bridge, and also began to cross it. He was a tall man with long limbs, and he was dressed in the rough homespun garb of a peasant. Twirling a great staff in his hands, he strutted toward Robin.

"Where are your manners, fellow?" Robin asked. "Saw you not that I was already on the bridge when you did place your great feet on it?"

And the other retorted, "The small jack should ever

give way to the big pot."

Robin, furious, ran off the bridge to cut himself a staff. Then he returned to meet the giant.

"Whoever is knocked from the bridge into the stream," said Robin, "shall lose the battle. Now, go!"

As their staves clashed together, both men knew they were well matched. Taking every step on the narrow bridge with great care, they fought on. Suddenly, Robin got in a blow on the big man's crown. But then, with a furious stroke, the stranger struck Robin off his balance, and with a mighty splash the outlaw fell into the water.

Robin pulled himself from the stream and shouted with a laugh, "You have got the day, big fellow."

The big man walked over to Robin. "What!" said Robin. "You were in so pesky a hurry to cross the bridge that you would not budge for me, and yet you do not go forward on your journey?"

"Aye," said the big man sheepishly. "I have not whither to go. But I would like to shake hands with you ere I wend, for you are as true and good a fighter as ever I met."

Robin's hand was in the other's big fingers at once.

"What is your name, good man?" he asked.

The other replied, "Men call me John the Little."

Robin laughed. "Stay a while, Little John, and sup with me." And Little John followed Robin to his camp, and supped with Robin and his men, and stayed for more than a while.

By the time summer returned, Robin's band had grown from twenty men to fifty-five, even though he had been in the greenwood but a year. His fame had spread quickly, and many who were suffering from hard and fruitless toil had run away to join him. Others, members of marauding bands of robbers, had been given the choice of joining Robin or fighting him to the death. They had chosen the safer course.

From the newcomers came tales of another dweller in the forest. It was said he was a hermit who was bold and independent, living in the greenwood by neither the king's laws nor Robin Hood's but only by his own. These tales excited Robin's curiosity, and one day he went south in search of Friar Tuck.

When Robin reached the hermit's hold, he walked about the area looking for Friar Tuck. He soon came upon the broad and sturdy monk, who sat silently beside a stream. Robin approached him and said, "Ho, there, holy man! I have business t'other side of the stream. Up and take me on your broad back, lest I wet my feet."

The big monk looked at Robin as if he hardly understood. Robin laughed.

"Up, oaf," he said. "Ferry me across the stream on your lazy back, or this arrow will tickle your ribs!"

Without a word the monk rose and bent his back before Robin, who got up on it. Then the monk stepped into the stream and walked slowly across the paved ford until he came to the other side. There he stepped up on the bank, and Robin prepared to jump off. But the monk seized Robin's left leg in an iron grip and gave him a great blow in the ribs on his right side. Robin fell backwards upon the bank. The monk, quickly pressing him down with one knee, placed great fingers upon his throat.

"Now, my fine fellow," said the monk, "carry me back to the place whence I came, or you shall suffer for it."

The monk then released Robin, and he, in spite of his rage, wondered at this. Why had the monk not beaten him senseless when he had Robin in his power? None would have blamed him. Already Robin regretted treating the monk with so high a hand.

Thus, without a word, Robin bent his back for the monk. Friar Tuck climbed upon Robin and allowed himself to be carried back across the stream. When the monk had been returned to the place from whence he came, he extended his hand to Robin Hood, whom he had recognized all along. And Robin took it respectfully for the first time, though not the last, for the two men were great friends ever after.

Before long it came to Robin's attention that his friend Alan-a-Dale had been declared an outlaw for aiding him. Alan was thus unable to do anything to save his love, Alice de Beauforest, from marrying the knight Sir Isenbart de Belame had chosen for her. The wedding was to be held soon.

On the morning the wedding was to take place, ten mounted men-at-arms wearing the livery of Ranulf de Greasby, the husband-to-be of Alice, rode up to her father's manor. The serfs who had been standing about scattered to make way for the fearsome group.

Another group of evil-looking men followed. This consisted of four knights, headed by Ranulf de Greasby. The old knight rode through the gate furiously.

"Hath the lady come yet?" he cried.

"Nay, lord," replied one of his men-at-arms.

Grinding his teeth, Sir Ranulf turned to a minstrel who stood beside his horse and asked roughly, "Who are you, knave?"

"I am Jocelyn, the minstrel, sir knight," replied the man, twanging his harp.

"Sing, then, rascal," said the knight.

And the minstrel began to sing. While he did, Ranulf de Greasby watched him closely. There was something odd about this minstrel.

For a moment, Sir Ranulf's attention was distracted by the arrival of the lady Alice. When he turned back to the minstrel, the man was nowhere to be seen.

"Where went that rogue?" he asked a companion.

"I know not," said the other.

"Find him," said Sir Ranulf. Then he bowed, for Alice and her father, Sir Walter, were now walking past him into the church.

Sir Ranulf followed Sir Walter de Beauforest and his daughter into the church and up to the altar. Of all the faces about, only those of Sir Ranulf and his men were gay. The unhappy priest prepared to do his duty.

Suddenly, from the gloom along the wall of the church came a movement, and a man stepped forth into the light of the candles which stood upon the altar. It was the minstrel, but now in his hand he bore a bow instead of a harp.

"This is an evil and unfitting match," he cried in a loud, stern voice. "Sir Ranulf, begone lest ill and death befall you."

With a gesture of rage, Sir Ranulf drew his sword and took a step forward. As he did so, a hum as of a bee was heard, and a short black arrow shot down and pierced his throat. Without a cry, he fell heavily to the ground.

The minstrel, who of course was Robin Hood, placed a horn to his lips and blew a shrill blast which filled the church with echoes. At that moment, the men-at-arms lifted their swords against Robin's men, who were now pouring into the church. The battle raged.

When Robin Hood had accomplished his mission and peace had been restored, Sir Walter approached him and said, "I thank you, sir outlaw, for saving my daughter from this ill-starred match. Yet the knights you have slain have powerful friends, and I doubt not their vengeance will be heavy upon us all."

"Aye," replied Robin. "Your daughter and the man she loves shall be wedded, and they shall dwell with me in the forest. If you fear assault by de Belame, you, also, may come and live with us."

Sir Walter thanked Robin but chose to remain in his home. Alan and Alice, however, joined Robin in the greenwood as soon as Friar Tuck had married them.

Much later, on a gray and dreary morning, Robin received a message from Marian's uncle, Sir Richard at Lee. Marian's father had died, and the lady was in danger of being seized by a lord who wanted her lands.

"Now," thought Robin, "the time hath come to take sweet Marian into my keeping. I will instantly set forth to Malaset and bring Marian back to the greenwood. Friar Tuck shall wed us, and she shall live in peace with me and my merry men."

For many years, Robin and Marian did indeed live in peace. King Henry had died, and his son King Richard

of the Lion Heart had gone off upon the Crusade. The king's chancellor, who ruled in his absence, had been driven from power, and John, Richard's brother, had taken control. With all the upheaval, the lords and prelates had little time to bother the outlaws.

Then all good men sorrowed to learn that their gallant King Richard had been captured and lay imprisoned in a castle in Germany. A vast sum was demanded for his ransom. In order to raise this sum, the people of the land were heavily taxed.

Robin, for his part, wanted nothing more than to see the king speedily freed. He now stole more often from the travelers and put half of what he took from them into a collection for the king. Also, Robin went about making sure the people paid their taxes.

Finally, the ransom was paid, and King Richard returned to England. There he learned from a faithful nobleman of Robin Hood's deeds on his behalf and that of others.

"Methinks this is no common man," said the king. "Almost it seems that he doth right in spite of the laws, and that they be wrong indeed if they have forced him to flee to the greenwood. I will see this man, and by the

favor of heaven I will make him my friend."

For many days, King Richard tried to find Robin Hood. But Robin would not be found. At last, one of the king's chief foresters had an idea.

"Sire," he said, "take four lords. Dress yourselves in monks' weeds, and then I will guide you to the road where Robin and his comrades do haunt, and I lay my head on it you shall see that rascal ere long."

One morning, after King Richard and his party had traveled several days, they were stopped by a tall man in Lincoln green.

"Stay, sir abbot," he said. "By your leave you must bide with me a while."

Robin whistled and was instantly backed by twenty men. He then asked toll of the king, who graciously gave all that he had.

"I thank you, sir abbot," said Robin. "Will you stay and dine with us in greenwood fashion?"

"Gramercy," said the king, "that I will."

After a hale and hearty meal, the men of the greenwood turned to their favorite sport. Targets were set up, and a number of outlaws began to shoot.

"He that doth not hit the mark," cried Robin, "shall

lose his bow and arrows, and shall bear a buffet from him that was the better archer."

Twice Robin shot at the mark and each time he cleft the wand. But others missed, and those who fell before Robin's buffet were many. Then Robin shot for the third time, and he was unlucky, for his bolt missed by the space of three fingers.

There were cries of "A miss!" and much laughter.

"I avow it," said Robin, laughing. Then he turned to the king. "I yield my bow and arrow to you, lord abbot. Now give me such a buffet as you can."

The king smiled, bared his arm, and gave so stout a blow on Robin's chest that the outlaw was hurled some distance and almost fell. He kept his feet, however, and approached the king to praise his strength.

At that moment, Richard of the Lion Heart thrust the cowl from his head and tore aside the black robes he wore, revealing the garb of the king of England. The outlaws fell to their knees.

"Rise, Robin," said the king, "for I have never met a man so much after my heart as you are. You must leave this life and be my liege servant and rule yourself as a lawful man."

"That will I do, my lord," said Robin.

"Go, then," replied the king, "take your fair dame and dwell with her on her lands at Malaset, at peace with my deer and all your fellow subjects."

The king then inquired of the deeds of the lords of Wrangby, of which he had heard but little. His brow went dark with anger when he learned of their wickedness.

"They are an evil brood," he said sadly. "But I and my dear father's other undutiful sons did bring them to life, for we plunged the realm in wicked wars and confusion. But let me settle with Philip of France. Then I will come back and sweep these evil castles from the land."

As the king had bidden him, Robin went with Marian to Malaset. With him went Hob, Ket, and Little John.

The rest of the outlaws followed Richard to fight in Normandy. Only a score or two returned after the king's death. All gradually drifted to Malaset, where Robin settled them on his lands. And there they stayed for many years, happy despite the terrible unrest that prevailed throughout the reign of King John and long afterward.